Old, Tired Dog

Contents

By Alison Lohans

Illustrated by Raymond McGrath

Old, Tired Dog

The Realization

Chris gave a hearty push and arrived at the top of the slope first. Then he had to wait for his dog. He restlessly rolled his skateboard forward and back again. Even at this distance, he could hear Ginger's harsh breathing from below.

Ian's skateboard rumbled on the rough surface as he came to a stop beside Chris. He, too, stood watching as Ginger plodded upward.

"That dog needs a wheelchair," Ian said. "She is the world's one and only canine tortoise."

Chris ignored his cousin's taunt. As the stiff old beagle hobbled up the path toward him, he realized with a sudden, sharp insight exactly what "doggedly" meant.

First Reading

What does Ian's description of Ginger tell you about the dog?

Close Reading

What words and phrases does the author use on page 2 to help you understand what Ginger is like?

Was it cruel of him, bringing Ginger along today? She had barked so excitedly at the front door when they left—and this meant he wouldn't have to walk her later. He and Ian had planned to see the latest Captain Xenos movie that evening. Just now, though, Captain Xenos and his space quests seemed like a tedious assignment. Or, was it Ginger who was the burden?

Chris kept his eyes on her, watching closely. She seemed to be favoring her left hind leg. Mom had recently mentioned that Ginger's hips weren't working well.

Chris tried to shut it all out. For as long as he could remember, Ginger had been part of his life. In some ways, nobody understood him or listened to him in quite the same way she did. At times, she almost seemed to read his mind, anticipating his every movement. Other times, she'd sit there, gazing at him with a look of sheer love in her golden-brown eyes. It wasn't something he wanted to discuss with Ian.

Dog tags jingled as the old dog dragged herself up the final stretch. Then she dropped onto the grass and lay there panting. Chris extended his hand and was shocked by the dryness of her nose.

Ian broke into his thoughts. "Seriously, why'd you bring her along? All she ever does is slow us down."

Chris shrugged. There were no pets in Ian's house because of Aunt Susan's allergies.

"She wanted to come," he muttered. "You saw her. Besides, she needs exercise."

Ian gave a shout of laughter. "That dog needs a fitness trainer. Can't you just see her, working the weights?"

The image that came to Chris's mind was the treadmill. He turned away so Ian wouldn't see his face.

Ginger recently had trouble getting in and out of the car. Stairs were hard, too. Chris slipped his hand into his pocket and slid his fingers over his compass, a gift from Grandad.

Close Reading

What problem has been introduced? Explain using details from the story.

First Reading

What is Ian's attitude toward Ginger? Why does Chris think Ian feels this way?

First Reading

How does the illustration support the action of the story?

A Dilemma

Ian set down his skateboard and pulled an electronic game from his backpack. "Your dad says she ought to be put to sleep," he said as the game beeped.

"You take that back!" Chris's fist clenched around the compass. Ginger was his dog . . .

He'd overheard several murmured conversations when his parents thought he was out of earshot. Words such as "merciful" and "kindest thing" kept coming up. Mom and Dad sometimes stopped talking when he entered the room.

"Well," Ian said, clicking his game. "She is old."

Chris knelt beside Ginger. A slurpy kiss to his nose brought a smile. He rumpled her ears.

Ginger's sides still heaved from the effort of climbing the slope. She gave a harsh cough, and tiny droplets were flung into Chris's face. He backed away. The dry, hacking spasms continued, like a sharp blade thrust into his gut. Ginger had been coughing for several weeks now.

The prescription from the vet obviously wasn't helping.

There was an explosion in Ian's game. "Drat," said his cousin, propping one foot on his skateboard. His fingers continued their relentless dance on the electronic device. "Coming?"

Chris didn't reply. Ginger was too tired to move. Her eyes had an awful glazed look.

Ian returned the game to his backpack and glided lazily for a moment on his skateboard. An instant later, he crouched and rocketed downhill.

"Hey!" Chris yelled after him. "Wait up for me, will you?"

He pushed off, unable to repress a murky feeling of guilt as his skateboard rumbled over the pavement and the wind whooshed in his ears. Ginger would have an easier time going downhill, he told himself. Besides, there were puddles on the street from last night's rain. She could get a drink of water . . . and then she'd feel better!

When he checked over his shoulder, the old dog was standing at the top of the slope, looking right at him. He could just hear her whine.

"Come on, girl," he called.

First Reading

Why does Chris feel guilty? What does he do to lose this feeling?

First Reading

Why does Chris leave Ginger and go with Ian? What does this tell you about Chris?

"Let's go to the mall," Ian said when they reached the bottom. "The new Captain Xenos game might be in." Without waiting for a response, he glided away.

Ian knew perfectly well that dogs weren't welcome at the mall. Swerving his skateboard in a wide figure eight, Chris wondered what he should do. If Ginger was picked up wandering stray, there'd be a hefty fine. What if she got hit by a car? . . . The rhythm of his clacking wheels punctuated his thoughts.

"Ginger!" he yelled. "Come!"

She didn't.

Frustrated, he pushed off and caught up with his cousin.

Ginger knew the way home.

The Search

In the electronics store, Chris was restless as Ian went from one game to another, up and down the long glass display case. The brightly colored boxes seemed oddly harsh. One had a picture of a skinny black dog with spiky ears and blue wings sprouting from its shoulders.

Clutching his skateboard against his body, Chris thought about Ginger, waiting where he'd left her.

"Hey, Ian, I'm going," he said at last. "I'd better check on Ginger."

Ian's nose was pressed to the glass. Chris suspected he wasn't even listening.

"I'm going," repeated Chris.

Ian shrugged. "Whatever. I'll see you tonight."

Close Reading

Compare and contrast the characters of Chris and Ian using details from the story.

Ginger was no longer at the top of the slope. Wildly, Chris looked in all directions. "Ginger!" he called. No old beagle came running toward him. There was no sound of dog nails on pavement or the faint jingling of dog tags.

With his heart in his throat, Chris took the long way home, trying to remember all the places that had fascinated Ginger during their many walks together. He saw a leashed poodle and a German shepherd out with their owners. He saw a black mutt exploring on its own.

There was no sign of Ginger . . . anywhere.

There was no dog waiting in the back garden when at last he returned home.

First Reading

How do Chris's emotions change from the first paragraph to the second paragraph?

Close Reading

How does the narrator's point of view influence how events are described?

They had fried chicken for supper. Chris only poked at it. He kept seeing the look in Ginger's eyes as he'd deserted her.

"Why so quiet, Chris?" Dad asked once.

"Just thinking about Ginger." A bite of mashed potatoes threatened to choke him.

Dad put down his knife and fork. "Son, we need to talk. I think it's time . . ."

"No. Now is not the time." Mom almost never interrupted, but this time she did.

"I'm not hungry," Chris said. "May I please be excused?" Dusk was setting in, and all he could think of was Ginger, standing there at the top of the slope.

Mom felt his forehead. "You feel a bit warm," she said. "Do you have a headache? Maybe you should lie down for a while."

Chris pulled away.

First Reading

What does Chris wish he could do? Why doesn't he do it?

His shoulders sagged as he went to his room. More than anything, he wanted to go out looking again—but, if he did, he'd have to explain why. He got his game and tried to lose himself in the darting images and flurry of electronic sounds.

Where was she?

Eventually, there was a tap on his door. "Chris," said his dad. "We'd like to talk with you."

Poor, Tired Dog

A feeling of dread clenched Chris's gut. Without speaking, he followed Dad to the living room. Ginger lay on the rug by the fireplace. Her eyes were dull and half-closed. Her throat gurgled in an alarming way. Chris's eyes filmed with wetness. He knelt beside Ginger and ran his hand along her back.

"Poor, tired dog." Mom's voice didn't sound right.

Chris drew in a deep breath. "She's not getting better." It came out sounding like an accusation. To his horror, a few tears streaked down his face.

His father's hand settled gently on his shoulder. Chris shrugged it away.

"Is she in pain?"

Chris's throat ached and, as he looked at Ginger, he knew the answer to his question.

He pressed his wet face against her. Her tail flopped limply, but she didn't move again, apart from the heaving of her sides with each ragged breath. He stroked the familiar, warm shape of her head, and then gently, both of her long, floppy ears.

First Reading

What happens when Chris begins to speak?

. . . poor, tired dog

Close Reading

Describe Chris's emotions. Include details from the text that helped you understand.

The shriek of the phone startled everyone. Dully, Chris listened to its intrusive bleating. Mom sighed and stood up to answer it.

"It's Ian," she said a moment later. "He says you two planned to see a movie together?"

"I'm busy," he mumbled. Earlier, he'd made Ginger wait. Well, this time Ian and Captain Xenos could wait. The film would be at the theater for several weeks.

"I'll call him tomorrow. Isn't that right, Ginger?" he said, stroking her head.

She gazed back at him with an odd, patient look. Her golden-brown eyes seemed to be asking him for something. It wasn't any of the usual things—food, games, or a car ride. This was different.

Suddenly, Chris thought perhaps he knew what it was.

"So what should we do?" he asked, gliding his fingers along Ginger's back, scratching all the places that made her feel good. When he rubbed her chest and stomach, the old dog gave a little sigh.

First Reading

What does Chris realize when he looks into Ginger's eyes?

"Well . . ." Again Mom's voice didn't sound right.

"She's suffering," Dad said quietly. "I'm sure you know that, son. Don't you think the kindest thing would be to put her to sleep?"

No! he wanted to yell. Ginger was his dog!

There had to be something else they could try—some new kind of medicine. Was that what Ginger wanted, though? That look in her eyes made him wonder. So sad, so tired, so . . . finished. He knelt there with his head close to hers.

"Would it hurt?" he asked at last. Immediately, he wondered if he'd betrayed her.

"No," said Mom. "Not any more than she hurts right now."

This time he didn't pull away from the gentle hand that came to rest on his shoulder.

Close Reading

What words does the author use to describe the sound of the phone? How do these words reflect the tension of the story?

First Reading

Why is the view outside described as "brutal beauty"?

Goodbye . . .

But they didn't have to take Ginger to the vet. She died late that night, curled up on the rug near the fireplace, long after everyone had gone to bed.

It was Mom who found her and Mom who woke Chris with the news. "Dad's going to bury her in the back garden," she said, once Chris had rubbed the sleep and sudden tears from his eyes. "Do you want to be there to say goodbye?"

Chris looked outside rather than at Mom's concerned face. None of it seemed real—the brutal beauty of a cloudless sky, green leaves fluttering outside his window, a chorus of birds rejoicing about something . . .

She was gone . . .

He sniffled hard, and then drove his fist into his pillow. Did he want to see Ginger's lifeless body, stiff and cold? Did he want to see Dad digging a hole in the dirt . . . and a familiar tan, black, and white form placed in it?

"Leave me alone!" he yelled.

Chris yanked the covers over his head. The suffocating darkness allowed him the luxury of tears.

Quietly, Mom left him.

Images flooded his head—an old beagle hobbling to keep up with him, a younger Ginger, dancing beside him with a smile in her eyes . . . and, occasionally, during quiet moments, a single haunting whimper of pain. Had he killed her?

The logical part of his brain insisted that she would have died anyway, but a condemning guilt lurked somewhere in his thoughts.

Chris stayed where he was, wishing he could be small again and curl up in Mom's lap. When Ian came around later, wanting to go to the matinée, he refused to get up.

First Reading

Reread the second paragraph. What does this mean?

Close Reading

Describe Chris's relationship with Ginger using details from the story.

Three days passed before he could make himself go out to the new mound beneath the oak tree in the back garden. He sat there a long time, listening to the hum of insects and the bird calls filtering through the branches. There was an ache inside that seemed as though it might never go away.

Was she happy now? Was the smile back in her eyes?

For a moment, it seemed as if Ginger's spirit was nearby, like an extra beam of sunlight dancing about his shoulders. Maybe wherever she was she was remembering him—just the way he would always remember her.

Close Reading

How is the problem, or conflict, in the story resolved?

Think about the Text

Which of the following connections can you make to the emotions, settings, situations, or characters in *Old, Tired Dog*?

Text to Text

Talk about other stories you have read that have similar features. Compare the stories.

Text to World

Talk about situations in the world that connect to elements in the story.

Planning a Narrative

1 Decide on a plot . . .

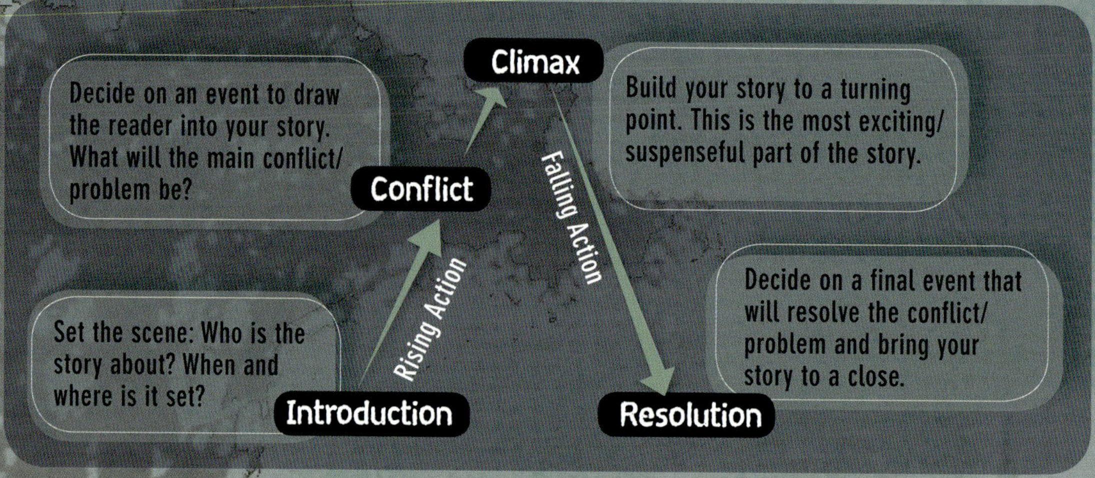

2 Think about . . .

- major and minor characters,
- how they think, feel, and act,
- their physical features, and
- their voice and their way of speaking.

3 Decide on the settings:

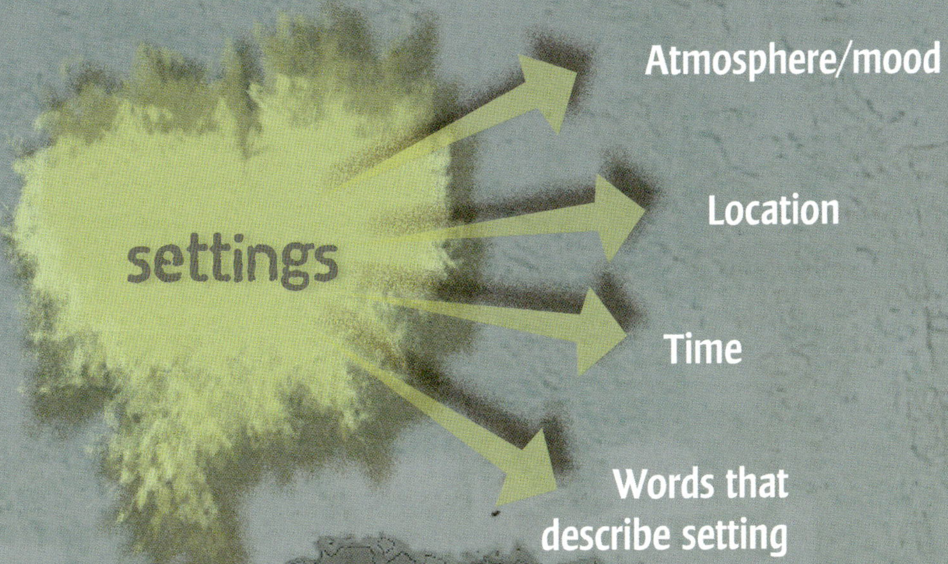

Don't forget . . .
to write your events in the order they occur!

Writing a Narrative

Have you. . .

- included an introduction that quickly tells the reader...
  - who the story is about,
  - where the story is set, and
  - when the story happened?
- included a problem (or problems) that makes the reader want to read on to find out how the problem (or problems) is solved?
- tried to create an emotional response within the reader?
- included description and dialogue?
- created mood and tension?
- included characters, settings, and moods that are connected to create a believable storyline?

Don't forget to revisit your writing. Do you need to change, add, or delete anything to improve your story?